I Can Read About™
PREHISTORIC ANIMALS

Written by David Eastman • Illustrated by John D. Dawson

Consultant: Dr. Niles Eldredge, Curator
Department of Invertebrates, American Museum of Natural History

Imagine a time millions of years ago, when dinosaurs and other prehistoric animals lived on earth. What was life like during prehistoric times? How did the creatures of the past live? Today, scientists hope to answer these questions by studying fossils.

Some fossils are bones or teeth that have turned to rock. Some fossils are shells. Others are marks and impressions, such as leaf shapes, footprints, or shell prints, left by prehistoric plants and creatures.

When scientists find fossils, they clean them and number them. They note where each fossil was found. If they find many bones in one place, they try to fit them together to make a skeleton.

Scientists divide the earth's history into time periods. Each period has a name. When scientists know how old a fossil is, they know during which time period the animal lived. Here are several time periods and some of the animals and plants that lived during each one.

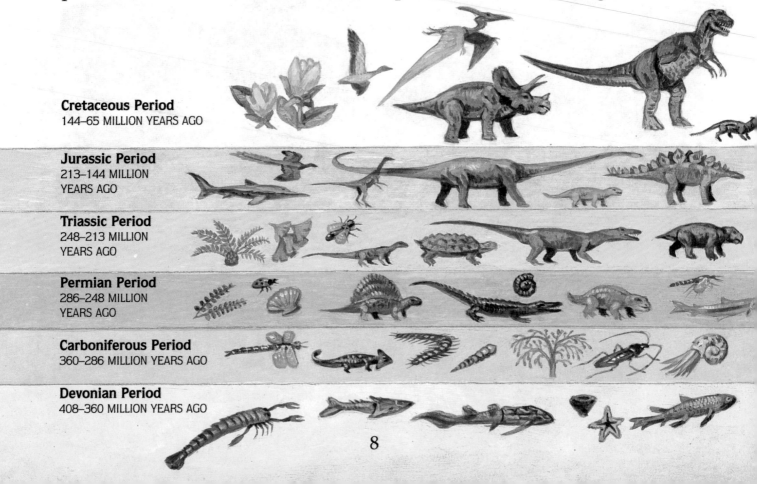

Cretaceous Period
144–65 MILLION YEARS AGO

Jurassic Period
213–144 MILLION
YEARS AGO

Triassic Period
248–213 MILLION
YEARS AGO

Permian Period
286–248 MILLION
YEARS AGO

Carboniferous Period
360–286 MILLION YEARS AGO

Devonian Period
408–360 MILLION YEARS AGO

There were many kinds of prehistoric animals. The first creatures lived in ancient seas. They were invertebrates (in-VER-tuh-brates). They had no backbones or spines. A jellyfish is an invertebrate. When prehistoric jellyfish died, they sometimes left fossil imprints in the sand.

There were also many tiny animals living in these long-ago seas. There were sponges, snails, and shell-covered animals called trilobites (TRY-la-bites).

Sponge

Trilobite

Snail

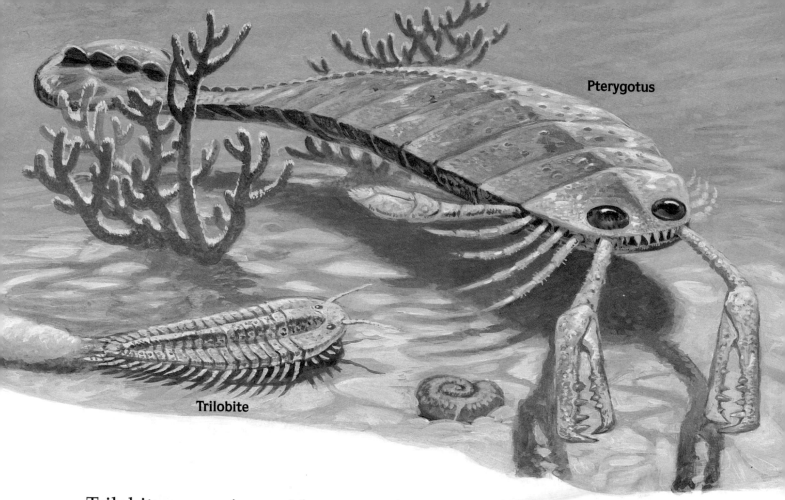

Pterygotus

Trilobite

Trilobites came in a wide range of sizes, from less than an inch (2.5 centimeters) to nearly 2 feet (61 centimeters) long. Giant sea scorpions that were almost 9 feet (3 meters) long also lived in the sea.

Some prehistoric animals looked like fish. They had backbones, but they did not have jaws. Instead, they had holes or slits for a mouth. They ate small plants and tiny animals.

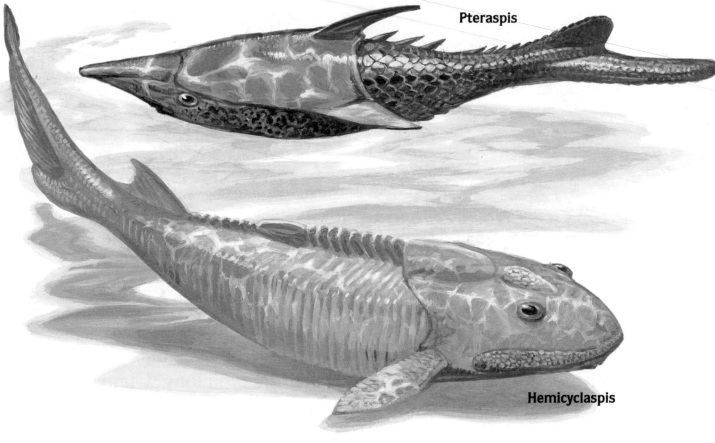

Pteraspis

Hemicyclaspis

Other fishlike animals had jaws. Some had armor, or hard plates of bone, and lived on the bottom of the ocean. Others had no armor but could swim very fast.

Dunkleosteus

Bothriolepis

Some early fish had skeletons made of bone. Others had skeletons made of cartilage (KAR-tih-ledge). Cartilage is a bonelike material, but it is softer than bone. Today's sharks still have skeletons made of cartilage.

Modern shark skeleton

Giant
dragonfly

Some of the earliest creatures to live on land were worms
and insects, such as giant dragonflies.

A fish like the lobe-fin (LOBE-fin) used its fins to crawl out of the water. Gradually, over millions of years, the lobe-fins evolved, or changed, into early amphibians (am-FIB-bee-uhns).

Eusthenopteron
(a lobe-fin)

Eryops

Young amphibians are born in and live in the water, like fish. But as they grow older, amphibians develop lungs and are able to breathe and live on land. Eryops (EAR-ee-ops) was an amphibian that lived 225 million years ago.

Seymouria

Prehistoric amphibians went through many changes. Some looked very strange. Scientists think that an animal like Seymouria (see-MORE-ee-ya) may have been an ancestor of the early reptiles.

Reptiles are born with lungs. They do not need to be born in water. They have an outside skin made of scales, or hard bony plates. Snakes, lizards, and turtles are modern reptiles.

MODERN AMPHIBIANS

MODERN REPTILES

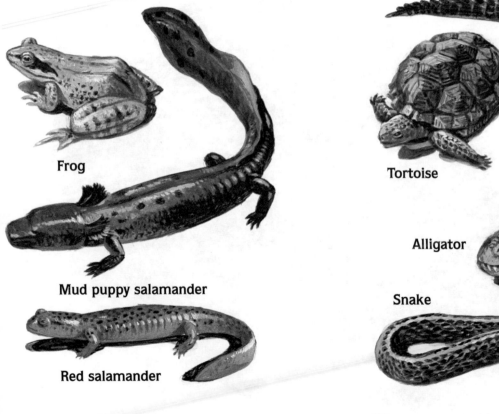

Frog

Mud puppy salamander

Red salamander

Tortoise

Alligator

Snake

Most of the early reptiles were not very large. Some were only 1 or 2 feet (30-60 centimeters) long. Certain early reptiles probably ate insects. Others ate plants. Some had sharp, bony points, or spikes, on their heads and backs.

Elginia

Hylonomus

Some reptiles were meat-eaters who preyed upon amphibians.

Cynognathus

Bradysaurus

Bradysaurus (BRAD-ih-sawr-us) was a plant-eater. This creature was 8 feet (2 meters) long and had claws on its toes. These sharp claws were probably used for digging plants.

Dimetrodon

Dimetrodon (dye-MET-ruh-don) had large jaws and very sharp teeth. This meat-eater was 10 feet (3 meters) long and had a 3-foot-high (1-meter-high) sail on its back.

As different kinds of reptiles developed, some looked like snakes with legs. Some looked like crocodiles. Others looked like lizards. And yet others looked like dinosaurs.

Tanystropheus

24

The Age of Dinosaurs began about 200 million years ago. There were many kinds of dinosaurs. Some walked on two feet. Some walked on four feet. Some ate meat, and some ate plants. Not all the animals that lived during the Age of Dinosaurs were dinosaurs. Some were reptiles that swam in the water or flew in the sky.

Brachiosaurus (BRAK-ee-uh-sawr-us) was among the heaviest of all the dinosaurs. Brachiosaurus weighed more than 89 tons (80 metric tons) and was 75 feet (23 meters) long. It had a long neck, and its front legs were longer than its back legs. This giant spent its time among the forests. It ate the tops of tall trees.

Brachiosaurus

Coelophysis

Early meat-eating dinosaurs were not very large. They walked on two hind legs and had short front legs.

Allosaurus (AL-uh-sawr-us) was big. This meat-eater was over 35 feet (10.5 meters) long. Allosaurus had strong legs and sharp teeth to hunt even the largest of the plant-eaters.

Time passed, and an even bigger dinosaur developed. It was Tyrannosaurus (tie-RAN-uh-sawr-us). This ferocious hunter was 50 feet (15 meters) long and 19 feet (6 meters) high. Tyrannosaurus had strong hind legs with claws, strong jaws, and teeth almost 6 inches (15 centimeters) long. These very sharp teeth could bite through bone.

Allosaurus

Tyrannosaurus

29

The duck-billed dinosaurs were plant-eaters. Fossil remains from their stomachs show they ate leaves, seeds, twigs, and fruit. Some duck-billed dinosaurs had high crests on their heads. These creatures walked on their strong back legs.

Iguanodon (ih-GWAN-uh-don) had hard, pointed claws. This creature was 15 feet (4.5 meters) tall and 25 feet (7.5 meters) long. When Iguanodon walked, it used its heavy tail to help it keep its balance.

Iguanodon

Some dinosaurs had armor for protection. Others had bones, horns, spikes, or hard plates. Triceratops (tri-SER-a-tops) had three horns and a bony shield behind its head. Ankylosaurus (an-KILL-o-sawr-us) had a plate covering and a tail like a club.

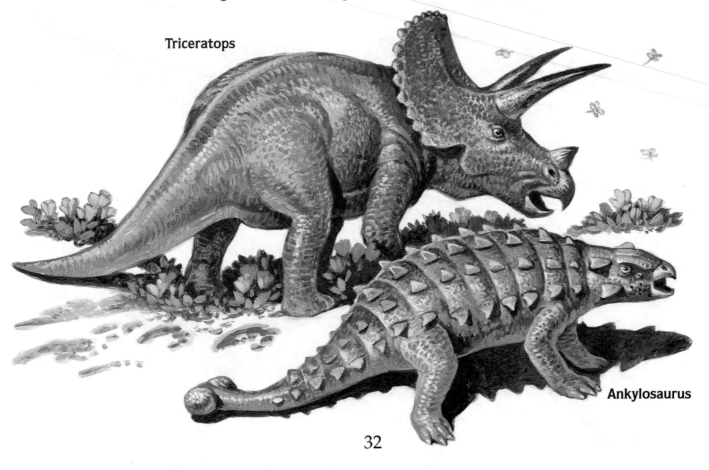

Triceratops

Ankylosaurus

Strange, prehistoric reptiles filled the seas. These huge monsters hunted their prey using their strong flippers and sharp teeth. Elasmosaurus (ee-LAZ-mo-sawr-us) had a neck like a snake and looked like a sea serpent. It was 43 feet (13 meters) long.

Elasmosaurus

Tylosaurus

Pterodactyl

Pteranodon

Archaeopteryx

During the Age of Dinosaurs, new groups of animals developed. Flying reptiles like the Pterodactyl (ter-uh-DAK-til) and Rhamphorhynchus (ram-for-RINK-us) had huge batlike wings. Pteranodon (ter-AN-uh-don) was another huge monster of the air.

Then another group developed. Scientists have discovered that today's birds are very likely related to dinosaurs! The 150-million-year-old fossils of a bird named Archaeopteryx (ar-kee-OP-tuh-riks) have been found. This creature had feathers and wings, but it also shared some features of the dinosaurs.

Ichthyornis dispar

Rhamphorhynchus

Hesperornis regalis

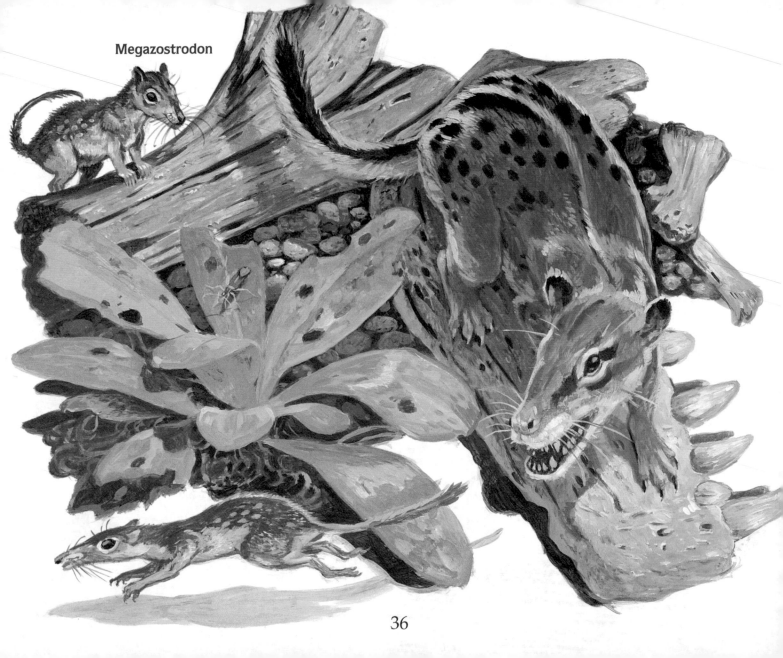

Megazostrodon

36

As the earth and its weather changed over millions of years, a different group of animals became important. They were the mammals. In the beginning, most were small. Instead of scales, they had fur or hair. Instead of laying eggs, they gave birth to live babies.

Opossum

Unlike reptiles, mammals were warm-blooded. The temperature of their blood did not change with the outside weather, as it did with cold-blooded reptiles.

Gymnogyps

Eobasileus

Brontotherium

Pliohippus

After the dinosaurs died off, the mammals grew larger and heavier. Some looked like tiny horses. Some had horns on their noses. Some looked like strange elephants, only smaller.

Synthetoceras

Mastodon

Later, mammals began to look more like modern animals.
There were huge mastodons (MAS-tuh-dons) with long tusks.

There were saber-toothed cats almost as big as modern lions.
Their strong, knifelike teeth were 9 inches (22 centimeters) long.

Saber-toothed cat

Mammoth

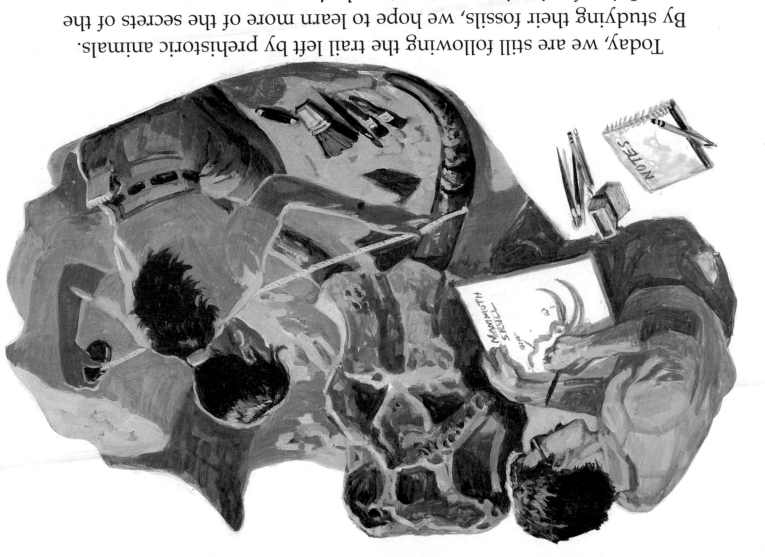

Today, we are still following the trail left by prehistoric animals. By studying their fossils, we hope to learn more of the secrets of the past. It is a fascinating mystery to solve!

There was someone who could think. There was someone who could tell a story for the world to know. But many mysteries remain.

But prehistoric people were more than hunters. On the walls of their caves, they drew pictures of the animals they hunted. In the dawn of history, there was a new creature.

The mammoth lived in Asia, Europe, and North America. It was over 14 feet (4 meters) high.

Scientists know that prehistoric people hunted the mammoth. They probably used spears made of wood, stone, or bone.